to the moon of my life,

thank you for your love.

it will live throughout

the pages of my soul.

-z.k.d

To Hold The Light

By Zachry K. Douglas

rainy days were made for books,

coffee, and getting lost in an

adventure under the blankets

i know wherever i go,
there is a chance of
me seeing you
there.

not in flesh and bone,
but memory.

and that is a slow
burning hell.

when your 3am nightmares become your

reality, you have to know when to breathe,

open your eyes, and wipe the sweat from

your face. for even the most haunting of

dreams allow you a chance to try again.

her bones are filled with a beauty
resembling a field of wildflowers.
a spectacle meant to be held by
someone who values love as
as she adores her
scars.

i want my next breath
to enter your mouth
and go down into your
lungs as if it is finally
home and knock
whatever taste you had
before completely out
so you can remember
how it feels to have
someone you love
never want to leave.

when you get tired
and the sky around
you has shattered,
you are still the
keeper of the
moon.

hold on to what you
have and piece
together what
you will need
to give it the
home it
rightfully
deserves.

i love you because you
are my best friend and
every breath i forgot to
take before meeting
you.

i love you because without
you, i am not any good to
anyone, and that's a bold
statement to make, but it's
true, because i knew the
me before you.

hope sleeps and it
dreams of becoming
a possibility one day.

fear teases it with
thoughts of never
making it.

her ability lies within
how she soars over the
clouds and laughs at
such a thing.

she wanted to be
beautiful for so
long that she
forgot she
already
was.

i tell her every day,
as many times as
possible until
she closes
her eyes.

even then i whisper
in her ear so her
dreams can feel
it.

she knew i meant,
because i was once
in love with the
moon before
marrying her.

i will always

search for your

soul first, before

i lay my eyes on

your nakedness.

let's get drunk off
the universe and
listen to each
other try to
describe the
feeling of
being
somewhere
you're not
even sure
exists.

long after the final breath

i take, i will incessantly

search for the moments

filled with everything that

is you.

in all honesty,
i'd rather keep
my eyes closed
forever and
walk this world
as a ghost than
know you are
under the same
sky without me.

i climbed onto your

smile and finally saw

a world's worth of

adventures that

needed to

begin.

my soul was meant to love yours.

you can yell by the way they mirror

each other's reflection without fear

of distorting the truth.

your silence is not a hush,

but a calming hand running

over my neck; massaging out

the pain and ache of over

thirty years of nightmares.

may the space i feel between us inspire me to
become better this year; a better man, friend,
writer, human, and lover. may this space teach
me how close you need to be with yourself
before giving it to someone else. may this space
create a place for two arms and a smile when it
has given its last lesson. may this space seek out
my demons and shine love on them, because we
must acknowledge the pain in order to heal
completely. may this space i find myself in, greet
me and allow my bones to grow stronger for the
adventures that lie ahead of me. make me feel
what you need and i will be a universe of emotions
that does not self-destruct, but only constructs good
energy around him. be gentle with me. for i am
merely paper; folding myself over and over in order
to find the correct symmetry it takes to survive the
fire.

with a grin only she could notice, he said,
"you terrify me."

laughing it off and squinting her eyes just
a bit, she asked, "why is that?"

inching closer to make sure his heart was
touching hers, he said,

"because you know all the secrets i've never
told anyone. not even myself. if i were to lose
you, i would lose more than my best friend.
i would lose every part of me that ever meant
something in my life."

when you love something or someone as much as i adore her, you learn the meaning of, "i do." not in the sense of exchanging vows or empty promises, but if it brings me back to you each morning and night, i do. if it means being able to look at you in any light, i do. if it means handing over pieces of me that have cut and mangled others, but you are still holding me, i do. if it means knowing your pain and heartache are safe to be shared within my own, i do. if it means staying with you in the moments we are us, i do. when you love a heart as precious as hers, you learn each skip and flutter is a way of synching with your own. when you love a soul as memorable as hers, you take the good and bad, because all of your life you have never experienced anything other than misery. when you love a constructed sunset like her, you see the world differently and value the way it makes you cry by being so goddamn beautiful, because you forget the times you had been alone. when you tell her these things and she doesn't run, walk with her and never let go.

i do, love you.

there are days where i can show you more and give
you more of what you deserve. there are days when
i can adjust the sun and place it where you need it
the most. there are days i feel unworthy of someone
like you, because i have gone so long without myself,
even though i swore i was still breathing. there are
days it's frustrating and i want nothing more than to
hold you so you know without a shadow of a doubt
you are the only thing that keeps me together. there
are nights i toss and turn, aching to be closer to you
when you are away from me. there are nights i see your
face and i kiss it with my soul for you to know that you
are every reflection which makes me who i am. there are
nights i could handpick the moon from the sky and give
it to you wrapped in stars and it's still not enough, because
the heavens don't deserve you. in this life we tend to forget
what truly matters the most, because we think we will
always have it when our feet meet the floor in the morning
to try and better or even replicate the day before. my heart
is a foreigner to my own body and forgets to open the cage
others have locked it in. you have been the one woman
who never asked to have a key, but merely a chance to
watch it beat outside the walls of my chest. at the end of
the day, we are given opportunities to make the ones we
love, feel loved, and that is the most rewarding aspect of
life.

you are my art.
you are my love.
you are my life.

you are everything
i have that i will
give back
through words,
actions, and
responsibility.

leaning in to kiss your lips, i lose my
soul to your touch. a soft pocket of
air rests between us, as we move
closer to the sound of our bodies
playing in the moonlight.

with you i have no name, but you speak
love into me with the way your hips sway
back and forth, like the breeze massaging
the waves.

i press my chest against yours.
my arms encircling your sunset.
my eyes walk back and forth,
tracing moments.

there's silence in our storm, and then
we cave in the room around us;

falling back into the earth we had just left.

we all struggle from time to time with
our lives, but it's within those moments
and days of feeling pain that we unearth
something powerful if we choose to push
through it all; perseverance.

it doesn't matter how far you go out to sea, as long

as your anchor is brave enough to stay strong and

hold you where you need to be.

the waves will never pull you away.

sometimes,
the greatest
adventure
is right in
front of
you.

just breathe and be thankful.

life is going to hurt you
someway, somehow
eventually.

you might as well live as
if it can't touch you and
see how far you can go.

what other people
say will never
matter,

unless you yourself
start to believe
what is
intended
for
someone
else.

and i will write everything i was born to say onto
your heart, limbs, and lips. making sure you
know exactly what i need when you read
the words every single day;

you and me.

maybe one day, everyone can experience this.
it is not only meant to be felt, but to be echoed
throughout the world; resonating in the bones
and souls of those who need it the most.

the pier has
walked itself
out to the
sea and i
followed the
pieces of
wood that
were
gathered by
the men
before me.
if you listen
closely, you
can hear the
stories of
how the
ocean
resides
in our
hearts.

you brought a kind of love into
my life that i've never tasted
before.

it's pure in every form and holds
together my reality in such a way,
even those around me feel
complete.

even hearts

float above

us in hopes

of finding

someone

to travel with.

there are times when you need to breathe and value

the quietness around you. even the hummingbird

needs to rest in order to find its next move.

the moon
and i are
friends.

she tells me
secrets that
i will share
with you
one day.

when the sky opens up and speaks about angels
and lost wings, you listen. life is nothing more
than chances; be it love, happiness, direction,
pain, or regret.

be brave in your adventure.

not everyone needs a hero. just someone who
can make them feel special and wanted.

it's scary at times not knowing what can
or could happen, but it's also scary
knowing.

whatever you do, don't be afraid of it.
at some point, all of what scares us,
creates us.

-start creating-

run with the wind
and you'll be able
to experience life
as it does;

    absolutely free and heroic.

swim in the waves and dance in the sand.
get lost in the sounds and allow them to
sweep you up in the ocean air.

be patient.

the best things in life
happen unexpectedly.

loving you, i have tasted eternity.
knowing you, i now have happiness.
seeing you, i now believe in the truth.

and the truth is, you have always been the
one. where we go from here is unknown,
but the adventure to get there and discover
a life with each other will always be worth it.

the layers of life
have been built
over time.

exuding the most
precious of gifts
during the
seasonal
change
across
the
horizon's
eye.

even in the clouds, my heart will always be yours.

the life i want to have with you, is the life i never

thought was possible years ago. i pictured being

alone because of the decisions made by myself.

now, a love grows wild amongst the dancing

souls of eternity.

home is where you go to rest your heart, mind,
and soul. i have a few places, but the ocean will
always be where i go to soak in the love of the
universe. it's a universal love kind of thing.
one of which washes me with the stars that
have fallen into the water over time.

    it's where i am unbound and
    where you can find me when
    it's my time to leave.

i've been kissed by the death of a thousand lives and still there is life inside of me. once where there was an empty valley without a running stream of hope, clouds of love build, and the downpour continues to replenish these dry bones and open soul.

rain on me with all you have.

i am ready to drown in it.

we will live and love by the sea.
a common place for lovers like
you and me.

just lay down a blanket and we
will use the moon for our light.

this is our place. a place where
fingertips trace lips and hearts
count falling stars.

a gate of love.
forever
locked by
two.
where
thousands
before us
have traveled,
just so they
could be
surrounded
by what has
escaped
them along
the way.

i long for the summer taste of the ocean like skies.

how with each wave that finds the shore, it reminds

me and brings me to closer to you. i do not have to

look far in order to realize your footprints lead out

into the sea. what a beautiful paradise it is for

mermaids to dance and just be free.

she was every

sunset i had

ever missed.

now, the sky

has never been

more beautiful.

today i feel like etching novels into the sky.
hoping we can read them together tonight
as the light of the moon shines on each
word that i have written for you.

chapter one: the day we met.

waking up and going to bed as one, will
always be what i love about us the most.

loving you and holding you, we are as
close as souls can be.

together, we are a connection of lovers
with a friendship that will never break.

though the patterns of life are monotonous at times,

it creates and builds the images of who we need to

be. looking past the glass of the human it reflects,

inside there is a wildfire of monumental strength

raging to engulf the untraveled maps of the

universe.

no matter how dark it gets, the signs will always
provide you with directions of which way you
need to go. stay strong and continue down the
road even if there is no light.

you would be surprised at how just one
candle can illuminate the entire sky.

we are all happening at once. our existence was not by accident. it is to meet those we need to and love those who understand the language our hearts speak.

listen closely and you will find the ones who enjoy a deep conversation about everything you are.

learn to take in the moments around you
and appreciate them while you are still
here.

the water is my solitude and the place i love to
go when the weather is as sunny and clear as it
is today.

even when it is not the case, i venture to the water
to feel the energy from the waves.

this is my element. this is where i belong.

she's the kind of light that
penetrates your soul and
finds the spots that
have been in the
dark far too
long.

it's under the moon when you will feel her the most.

dear beam of wonder,

you don't need permission to grow.
start where your wings feel free.
seek, breathe, and repeat.

beat for me,
with a heart
made of
promise and
intent on
being mine,
when i am
unable to be
my own.

come to me with your faults and fears,
and i will cover you with my love and
tell you how beautiful they are.

in life, all we need is for someone to
gather us from time to time so we
can find ourselves again.

i could tell the question was dancing on her tongue as if it
had been waiting for the stage to clear. she said, "do you
ever see us becoming more than what we are now?" it was
not the question i was expecting, but most of the questions
tend to be that way. those are the ones that give truth to
your feelings. i looked at her as if she was the first sunrise
i had ever relished in my life, and said, "what we are now,
i never knew could be a reality. if you're asking me do i
believe in us, i do. if waiting is what keeps us from being
more, then i will wait until these words become you.
i'll write my entire life until every sentence is your breath
and ever word becomes your touch. we are the beginning,
middle, and end to whatever we create. but the truth is,
i just want to keep reading with you until we compose
another book of us."

i know last night was restless for you. i was talking to

the moon about you again. i'll try not to boast about

you too loudly tonight, because i know how much

you love your sleep. but i am so damn proud of you

and she was being persistent about hearing what was

in my heart. forgive me, sweet one, some things can

never be talked about enough.

i am a simple man who wants what he cannot hold at this moment. i want our souls to merge and our bones to melt together. i want my skies to fill with the sunsets in your eyes so i can fall in love with from a distance when we are not touching. i want to close my windows and your voice be the last thing i hear before my dreams capture it again. i want you to consume me, so i can become a part of you. allow me to live in you and i will finally be at peace. i am learning how to spend a lifetime without the presence of you in the physical form and its teachings are providing me the words i never had the courage to say to anyone. i will continue to feel you in ways that let me know that i am still alive. as long as this ache exists, i know i'm getting closer to exploring your mind, body, and spirit.

i think about you often and dream of days where
i don't have to hang up the phone anymore or roll
over and you not be there. i think of the days where
we can take the moon and hold onto it as we go to
our place. how we can watch the sun and play with
the shadows it makes. i think about the days to come
and where you and i will be when we no longer have
distance between us, but only souls to shake. i think
about you often and i know one day this will all make
sense and why having each other this way is better than
being without the water we so desperately need to drink.
i think about you often and how it would be if you were
here holding me. my head in your lap as you read your
book and sip your tea. i think about how my hands would
feel on your thighs as you began to open them slightly just
because i made you move by running my fingertips up and
down your leg, trying to feel your pain and make it go
away. i think about how someone like you could

ever love a man like me, when all my life this man found
it difficult to even love himself. i think about you often
and more so when it's quiet, because even in the silence
i can still picture your lips as they form to speak my
name. i think about the way your heart feels on my chest
as i play with your hair and tell you, i love you. i think
about the lazy days we would have where we both are in
pajamas and neither of us feels like getting out of bed.
i think about you often and how my dreams never sleep
when they're constantly being reminded of the way you
mean to them. you are a place in time and space where
everything stops for a moment and within that second
of inspiration, life and i agree that when you truly love
someone, you become everything you thought was lost
by finding it in the little things. we are the moments,
my love, gone or forgotten, and we are here to be
remembered now for what we went through to finally
experience how the universe works behind the scenes to
bring galaxies together after being merely dust and bones
for so long.

i get jealous because i'm afraid you'll find something better than what i can give you. i am terrified of admitting to this, but i believe there is power to be lost if my heart gives into these thoughts. it's not easy writing this for you to read, but honesty is a drink never fully appreciated until it's gone, and then you have to chase lies for the rest of your life with an empty glass you no longer can hold because the weight of your sorrows are pulling you down behind the night. in this reality, you are only one decision away from a completely different life, and i will always bare my wounds to you and show you the spots where i've been the hurt the most. it's okay to be vulnerable and to feel everything, but once you stop, you will never appreciate the thought of losing someone or something you won't find again. i know, because it was once my death sentence i survived by stepping back form the light which tried to take me. several years later, i found your welcoming arms after searching for myself, and now i can see we have identical scars in the same spots.

there's poetry floating out of her head again and her eyes can sing the saddest songs. there's chaos in her heart and she's moving the stars around to create the art she needs. she's a born again rebel with wild underneath her fingernails. she will die trying to be where she is supposed to be, before conforming to any of your ways or beliefs. ashes fall from her wings as she prepares for another battle for her sanity. her lungs expand and her eyes widen right before she goes in for the kill. when you have been counted out all of your life, you learn how to evolve from being the underdog, to becoming the champion of all things worth fighting for. we are what our hearts scream out when no one else is listening. but after a while, everyone feels your fire.

my love for her killed off any
memory my demons tried
to hold on to.

the greatest cure for the pain,
is someone who heals you by
loving you for who you are.

it literally brings tears to my eyes wanting to do so
much for the ones i love, but not having the ability
to do anything about it. call it an excuse and i will call
you a liar, because my life is unknown to most. i want
to take my dad to napa so he can taste the nectar from
the gods and show him the valleys where they grow the
grapes. i want him to see the sunset and how it bounces
off of every bottle being poured. i want him to smile,
because it's been too long since my old man has been
happy. he deserves so fucking much and here i sit,
writing about it with hopes of making something out
of myself before it's too late. i want to take my mom to
paris,because she hasn't seen anything beautiful for so
long and has been working her bones down to dust for
the past seventeen years. she deserves to smile, because
it's been too long since i saw her happy. i want to take
my little brother to new york city, and show him what
art looks like when it's done by the lonely. he has had
a rough life and deserves to smile, because he has gone
too long without showing it off to people who need to
see how it has helped everyone feel better. i want to
take my older brother to california. the last time we
were there was nine years ago for my boot camp
graduation. there wasn't enough time to soak in
the ocean and give the sand a feeling of freedom.
he deserves to be happy, because he works his ass
off to provide for his family and he is the

most unselfish person i know. writing this, i'm in tears
because i feel them all the time and know how hard they
each have had it and i take responsibility for not being
able to do more, because i've protected each one for so
long, i have become a parent in a sense to my own family.
these tears being released, makes me have peace about it,
and each one that falls is another opportunity to let it all
happen and create another poem. i am an emotional
thunderstorm with sights and sounds resembling the lost
child i used to be. now i'm a grown man who still needs
help and never asks, but is beginning to see the bigger
picture of taking responsibility and owning my actions,
when for too long i acted out and drank myself into feeling
nothing at all. i'm misunderstood and bruised by lightning.
i'm a paradox of abandoned boxes filled with memories
and abilities to feel the slightest of eyes looking at me.
i want my family to know that i care and sometimes tears
only get you so far, but they are words i can never find.
i cry to find my way through the darkness. i cry to find
peace within the chaotic mess i am. for they have gone
too long without knowing anything other than pain.
i'm changing my life by becoming my own person.
don't stand next to me if you're afraid of showing
emotions. my life and the ones in it deserve to see
how it is you care, when they are hurting without
saying a goddamn thing.

i hope in my next life i can make you laugh more than
you cry and not be the pile of nerves around you. days
get lonely without your hand in mine, but i smile as if
i have finally found the cure for the stars crying out
inside of me. i knew i loved you when my scars turned
into stories i wasn't afraid to tell. from this point forward,
your love will be safe with me, as i gather the universe
around you to protect your innocence and save you from
the thought of being alone. i want you to remember me
as i am right here beside you, standing for every mountain
that ever fell before us. time is nothing more than a way of
showing how much you miss someone when the sky gets
heavy and can no longer keep you upright by simply telling
you, "it will be okay." i have always been weary of humans,
because they have a habit of leaving things they say mean
everything to them, and since i have met you, the only
thing that frightens me, is never finding you again if it
should come to that. i held out my arms as if they were
a bridge to hold your light, and i felt you cross over to me.
after that, i knew i was no longer the man afraid of the
monsters behind his eyes. we graciously became lovers of
the madness we once used to cover our faces to keep the
world out. together, we will welcome each other into a life
of promises we both want to grow old keeping.

it hasn't been the easiest of days and she came to me and asked if i could write something for her to keep the smile from completely falling off of her face. i opened my chest, grabbed my heart, and pulled it out just for her. i told her, "this is the only thing i've ever wanted to give someone and the only thing that is worth the words you will find inscribed in each marking you'll see. it has your name and a promise to be there when you feel the ground trembling beneath you and life doing its best to make your nerves turn into electric skies around you." i have never looked at another woman the way i do with her and it feels like my eyes were born to see her this way and every other way she presents herself. never before have i been able to press my soul against someone and hear the sounds of tomorrow in her release. when handling magic, never let go of the promise to be there, because once you lose it, nothing will appear the way it was before.

you are my favorite part of every day i get to see. i am
honored to know you, but even more thankful for your
love. it has shown me that there is nothing else like it or
you in this world, and to me, that's the greatest feeling
one can come to know while trying to find themselves.
it tells me it's okay to be who i am. it tells me it's okay
if i don't have everything figured out, because it doesn't
need to be anything more than us and nothing will ever
take away how i feel for you. it has taught me to trust
myself and by doing that, it's been the first time i can
honestly say i've done that without thinking about
anything else that has weighed me down. do i get
depressed, sometimes. do i get angry and frustrated at
my situation, sometimes. do i get scared that i'll never
hold you for the rest of my life whenever that time
comes, sometimes. but what we are and who we have
been will change the way days are counted until then.
i don't need anything more than your love, and if we
happen to finally come together one day and live with
the elements that life provides, it will be the greatest
day of my life. if we happen to fall more in love with
each other, each time we touch, it will be the greatest
feeling i will ever know. if we happen to promise each
other we will live for the other and spend our days
creating a life together, then i can tell

you that wherever we go and however it is we arrive to
where we need to be, love will always be present in every
word we speak. we are only here for a little while before
we meet someone who makes forever seem like it's not
long enough and how a breath feels when it's not your
own, when you had been alone for an eternity, holding
everything back. you are each day i want to live. you are
every month i want to rename. you are every year of my
life i wish to never count. you are every reason why i am
living now. you, and you alone, have the power to hold
shards of glass and make something entirely new again.
that's what you've done with me, sweet one. you make
me, me, and there's a space in-between each heartbeat
that says your name with such conviction that even my
blood knows the color of love. we are important,
because we choose to make each day a priority of
finding one another again when our hands are
searching for the other. no matter how far reality
tells us we are apart, there's no substituting free
will to decide what drives us to seek out the best
in ourselves and who we want helping us make
that decision.

before there was a you and me, our hearts had been longing to meet. the universe placed the sun in my chest and wrapped it with flesh and bone, knowing only you could set it free. and you, my love, you had the moon placed in your chest, wrapped with honey and love-soaked roses. we are of the same time and place, but lovers do not always spend a lifetime together.

it's a good thing the earth has yet to forfeit a turn for us.

you are my drive
you are my focus.

you are each breath i take in to be closer to you.
you are my reason for writing each letter in a way
that only you can understand. i want you to know
me more than anyone else in this world. i want to
hold you against me so you can hear the sounds of
my soul. you are the love of every star born in my
sky. you give me hope that i can succeed in this life.
you are the veins that carry blood to my heart.
you are the arms i never want to be without.
you are the hands i want to study more of to
know what gentle and loving feels like. you are
every waking second of the sun and every watchful
eye the moon sees with. you are a woman of purpose
and action. you are the only one in a sea of forever i
wish to swim with. you are my skin, my bones, and
my existence. i'll love you with more than the words
i try to put together to show you how much that is.
i'll love you until my wrinkles are all that's left of me
and my eyes finally shut for good. i'll love you with
each opportunity, gesture, and step in becoming who
i need to be for us.

with a single tear forming in the corner of my heart, utterly afraid of how a single sentence has the ability to kill you, i asked myself, "how will i know if she's the one?" i tend to talk in silence most days. it's hard to carry a relevant conversation with anyone except one or two people i know, so i find it therapeutic to see what my soul has to say. i closed my eyes, held my breath and heard, "if she helps you let go of the breath your bones just took hostage, you will know. if she lets you breathe with her, then you'll know." in a matter of a few rotations of the earth, she and i both learned how holding onto each other made more sense than walking this universe alone. it's more than a friendship. it's more than just love. it's about us finding comfort in an uncomfortable world that seems incredibly empty when you say goodnight and no one is there to say it back to you. now i have my sweet dreams and a woman who keeps my pieces together when the night used to come by and collect them to make mosaics on the wall, using my fears and failures to keep me up.

there's a star in your
chest that never asks
for attention.

it only asks not to be
judged, but loved for
the light and not the
way it is seen by those
passing by for a quick
glance.

i don't want perfect.

a seven letter word has never been more of a
death wish for so many before me. they say it
without seeing there's nothing beautiful about
perfection. there's no mess to clean up.

there's no one getting dirty to try and funk up their life.
there's no heart in the word, only misconceptions.

it's how we get lost, and trust me, there are more strange
and wondrous ways to get to that level.

i don't do perfect.

-i do honest-it's amazing what can happen when a single soul is

able to see what a mirror never could just by feeling

the pain growing from the soil others had buried it

in. you've always had permission to witness yourself

rise.

it's about time you start believing in your power.

she tastes like moonlight even during

my darkest of days. her breath allows

me to know i am alive, and that is all

i need in order to exist and belong to

something greater than myself.

go if you must, but continue loving the unstoppable
madness that lives inside of those wings. you are the
kind that sleeps quietly, whose dreams are as loud
as the ocean opening its eyes. you are the kind that
never asks for anything, but takes what they need with
such grace, those who oppose you will be left powerless
by an unforgettable face. we are a world of rules, but you
are a raging force of the unknown. you are the very reason
why we live and die for our beliefs to never anchor off
while having sails for souls.

she breathed earth into me
and covered my rugged
bones with life i had
been dying for.

soul to soul, we grew
and became a mystery
to a life who thought
it had everything
figured out.

i rose from the ruins of my own brokenness.

there were bones, heartache, shattered bottles,

empty faces, secondhand chances, and lifeless

poetry all over the place i once called home.

i now live with the wanderers who never settle

for anything that doesn't make us crawl out of

our skin to be closer to the impossible. in every

direction there are possibilities of greatness

projecting from the dreams we once kept under

our pillows as kids.

she's smiling again,

> and there's nothing more beautiful
> than a woman who knows who she
> is after being told all of her life,
> this is not for you. it's how heroes
> are made, and she's that to everyone
> who meets her.

be with someone who corrects you with love,
not anger. raising anything but your kindness
will always lead you down a path of unforgiving
actions.

when someone wants the best for you, they show it
by listening to you and hearing everything you don't
have the words to say.

they will never harass your effort or validity as a human
being. confiding in them, brings out the real you.

wherever you find yourself today, i hope they understand
you when there is enough silence in the room to suffocate
your bones.

-i hope they know how to hold
everything in place just for you-

beautiful girl,

       never stop skipping stones across those
rivers. one day, your pockets will be
empty and you will feel messy and out
of tune, but if you keep going, there are
waters where you can wash the fear from
your soul and turn it into wine to toast to
those who told you nothing was out there
for hidden secrets that don't know themselves.
sometimes, it's when you're alone that you
are the furthest thing from lonely and able
to be at peace with the truth.

i close my eyes and i have a single vision of your dreams.
we are travelers full of stories to tell, and when the day
hits us, we become the things we believe from the night
before. it is when you are away that my lungs seem to
fail me and i am left choking on my insecurities.
i honestly believe learning how to be near you, without
having you, is teaching me how to hold you better when
the time calls for us to be together. we must be willing to
accept that we are more than humans and must take in
how the sky feels when it only has half of the moon,
instead of every phase. single-handedly, we are capable
of generating a breath for someone a thousand miles
away. as long as you're alive, fight for each one that
epitomizes your love for them. the distance may never
close, but you will come to know who you are and what
you want when your ribs begin to open up for another
dance with the wind.

she's having a hard time putting words
to her life right now, but if all you can
do is just sit with your eyes on her,
do that. she won't tell you she needs
help, because she's not that kind of
woman. stay with her and grieve a part
of her life she is finally moving on from.
we must learn how to drop all of the fear
and try again. you need to see how the
leaves fall for you and understand that
healing is worth the work it takes.
it's okay to grow slow, but stunting your
soul for someone who would rather cut
you at the knees will always be what
keeps you from your potential.

once you let go, you'll
see how revolutionary
it is to carry yourself.

some days i barely have enough strength
to keep my body upright and buoyant.

other days i hope what's left can be
enough for you when you're in need
of my love. i will go where no one else
has gone for you, if it means my best
days live inside of you.

my heart had been a grave, full of death in every

corner, then you came along. you managed to

plant your love and give me all the sunshine

needed to be born again. now, my soul is a

rose garden that we both walk through

together.

we are only as soft as our hearts, but we were never
made to break. we are pain, love, madness, and
strange, waiting to introduce ourselves to
someone we have yet to meet.

to the women who have broken their
backs so others could have the honor
of standing up for what they believe
in, thank you for being a voice in
today's society.

> let it be thunder.
> let it be love.
> let it be a hurricane.
> let it be you.

speak for the stories that have been silenced.
to the little girls running around, looking for
heroes and role models, this world is yours.
unity is a choice, and however you choose to
enliven your heart, and the hearts around you,
be you, bravely.

you can let go of the pain, but sometimes it holds
on because it knows it cannot go on without you.
expand your lungs, embrace the uncertainty, and
make beautiful things out of it.

i have seen tears change the
world, so i know what you're
after is possible.

i hate not saying goodnight
to you. my soul never seems
to sleep and my demons turn
my mind into a revolving door;

-tirelessly spinning without peace-understanding why we are here may be the most difficult thing to do. but i promise you, if you always hold your heart with two hands and listen to its music, you'll always have something no one else ever will.

and sometimes, that's all we need to know.

you may feel too much. you may think too much.
you may exist more than those around you, but
continue speaking your consciousness and taking
care of the good in you. people might not
understand what you're made of, but
when you have a stubborn heart,

love cannot help but to fall for you.

chaos creates the most
beautiful disasters at
times,

and even then, your eyes
are filled with sex from
the stars.

it's called breaking for a reason, but learn the difference
in the way it can be used. BREAK for the breath you have
trouble finding. BREAK for the love you have difficulty
giving yourself. BREAK from the norm and grow for
once, instead of regressing and retreating back to the
old footsteps that have swollen your bones with regret.

we must give ourselves a chance
to feel that we are worthy of the
same affection by someone who
wants nothing more than to tell
us it's okay to be yourself, and
still love you for it.

we at times fall in love with
those unattainable, because
we know deep down, there
is a chance for a love greater
than what's around us.

the sky is filled with questions the universe attempts to
answer by using lessons to teach you what you need to
know. please remember that it never forgets a face it
has sculpted through pain. all art is precious and
sometimes we don't understand it, but we have
the power to love even through the cracks

last night i lost both my religion and faith in all things
i once thought i knew. but when i woke up, i was still
on my knees as you rose with the horizon. for you and
only you, will i lose it all, only to have your love lift me
up to where my mind can't take me. for you and only
you, will i promise to synchronize the wild which lives
inside of us both. i will take my time and add it to the
minutes i have been without you to make sure you
fully understand what it's been like dying of a love
i never thought i would discover.

she took my hand and without knowing it all,
took me to a place i had never experienced
before. to a feeling i had never felt more
honestly. to a region of my soul never
before explored. all at once she gained
my trust, because she told me as she
held my hand, "i love you and and
will make sure this hand i am holding
goes wherever i go." there's not a more
glorious way to burn for something than
with another person you want to travel
the world with, loving for the rest of your life.
it's amazing how quickly the memories add up
and are sketched all over your heart. each one a
footnote to a story forever being told.

open your hands and let go of the worry you hold onto,
squeezing the very life out of yourself. you need to be
kind to the love you offer. not everyone will value it
and that's why it's so uniquely yours.

when the moon is

hiding behind your

fears, hold out your

hands and look for me.

this year, open yourself up to more love from your own words and actions. be prepared to stay for as long as it takes to see the process through. continue opening up to everything you once thought you would never need and learn about the things you once thought were a waste of time. it's imperative you continue drowning in yourself until you learn that you do not need someone to save you. we are the sea, shore, and where everything meets and begins again. nurture yourself and always be accountable. once you lose respect for who you are, you invite everyone to treat you the same.

i started reflecting on the pain i once felt and came to the conclusion it was self-induced. no one has ever hurt me more than i did. somehow i got it twisted around my heart that someone else caused the disaster i am still trying to clean up. i have been apologizing to myself ever since i woke up in a hospital bed, not knowing where i was. today, i finally accepted my apology.

years will pass and people will leave you, but if you never abandon yourself, the pain will become a love you never knew you were capable of projecting. when you get to that point, shine it on everything you can. we all could use a little more if we are being honest with ourselves.

the life around me has changed, but your eyes

still tell me secrets i have been looking for

since the universe gave me your name.

i'm a madman in love with a moon who doesn't know
her own powers and how she moves me without doing
anything except remaining beautiful despite the darkness
around her. aliens like me aren't supposed to be with
something so extravagant and promising. i don't know
how i'll ever be able to keep you, but i promise i will
always hold you above the world on my shoulders.
there will be no greater feeling in my life than having
you be my eyes and heart when they both are blinded by
the struggle of trying to fit in where you don't belong.
i'm different, but at the same time, still wanting the same
things from life we all believe in. when i saw your moonish
tendencies, there was no turning back, and that will be the
story of our life together if you wish to live it with me.
the truth is, i know if you say no and leave the sky above
me, the weight of the world will become heavier, and i'm
for certain i will fall with it.

you have too much love to be left without anything to
speak of. your eyes tell me you're afraid, but the heart
of a lion never worries about finding the next day. it is
brave enough to survive the night alone if needed, but
before the sun makes a sound, there is victory in its jaws.
believe that this is where you were meant to thrive and
become each breath given out by the stars guarding the
night. you are here, and that is all you need to know
about your purpose. surrender those doubts you've been
carrying about yourself, sweet one. you are not only an
inspiration, you are the epitome of all things worthy of a
fresh start. we get so caught up in worrying about failing,
that we forget how it feels to be adored for trying. even if
it means nothing to anyone else, you are deserving of being
told, "i am proud of you."

please never forget, i always will be.

don't forget your wounds and why you bled to get to
where you are now. no matter what happens, you're
only a dream away from a new beginning. it's okay if
you're still learning how to love. countless people
believe they already do and discover themselves in the
trunk of their own hearts, wondering how many bodies
can actually fit inside and live comfortably. know your
bones and where they are best suited to grow if you
want a meaningful and happy life. smile at yourself.
laugh as ridiculously loud as you can. be the person
that makes you forget all of the terrible things that
have happened to you. what i'm trying to say is, fall
in love with who you are now. once it happens, you
will find that it's more difficult to give yourself away
to the wrong people.

-never forget, always protect your wild-

there's a reason why you feel the way you do. either you're
afraid, stuck, or where you think you are supposed to be
for now. take time to give thought and love to yourself
despite your predicament. one day, i will ask you how
you got to this point and i want you to be able to tell
them that nothing will ever be as rewarding and difficult
as the day you find out you have a choice in how your
journey goes and when it begins. we create our own finish
lines, and for some, they chose not to cross it because they
begin to explore the rest of the course and figure out that
your greatest memories and moments are made by the
unknown. it takes patience, and if you don't have any,
learn from those around you who stayed with you
throughout your highs and lows. anyone can do the
happy medium with you, but as we all know, life can
be anything but that. being alive demands your full
attention, and if you aren't willing to give yourself
that, nobody else is going to try differently for you.

one of the best feelings is realizing you're not the only one who feels fucking crazy after going through all of what you went through. the common misconception tossed around by people is that we all experience things differently, which is true, but what we forget is that collectively, we will encounter the same bullshit along the way and it's somewhat rewarding not being alone after your world implodes. there are only a few options you have after such a traumatic event occurs: pick up and build, or continue demolishing everything you see because life wasn't fair to you. when you wake up tomorrow, this place will have already changed from the day before, and it's your opportunity to allow yourself a chance to succeed by understanding life happens to all of us, and if you feel a bit off, chances are you will meet a few who live the same way. keep an eye out for your kind. they will seem familiar to you, because strangers don't exist when you're dealing with what is hurting you the most. spill your guts into the streets and you will discover you're not the only one bleeding from existence. if you don't find them, they will find you. some of us were made to feel the pain of others, and for that, i am grateful. it has given me courage to withstand my own breaking point.

i have to be this way. how else would others know who i
am if i cannot be me? how else would they know it's okay
to wake up from wounds of yesterday as the reason you
want to help heal others? how else could i love myself if
i'd never had an opportunity to lose someone else?
i have to be this way. there's nothing left for me if there
is not a chance to find myself again in a place i've never
been and a friend i haven't met yet. how else would i
know how to be whole if i've never lived in fractions of
time and space? i have to be this way. what's left of a man
who holds the scissors, only to have cut off his own hands
to give others more of what they need and never ask for
them again? how else would others know how to replace
what you thought you could never get back? i have to be
this way. we are nothing without being ourselves and if
that is too much to ask for when i need it, then don't
bother giving me anything you have to offer if you can't
afford to provide me with truth of who you are and what
keeps you from being more than just another tragedy
acting in front of empty chairs in a room you designed.

she never overindulges, but binges on the moments filled
with laughter and lighthearted cravings for a little more
than what she reads about in the books under her bed.
there you will find her secrets. there you will find journals
filled with who she is. the type of girl who lets the windows
open to smell the universe at night as the rain eases her
aches. there's something so subtle yet powerful about an
innocent heart. it proves you don't have to be who they
say in order to create magic around you. the kind that lies
awake and believes tomorrow will be better, regardless of
how many pages have been written describing the
tumultuous atmosphere she's breathing in. underneath
her body lives the greatest story ever told, and one day,
the monsters will be held captive by the woman who
feared her limitations, only to become limitless with her
ability to develop into who she needed back when they
told her, "i will always be here."

there comes a point in each cycle of our yearly dance
with the sun that we learn something new. something
painstakingly real and honest. we finally open up to
ourselves and speak directly to the source who is meant
to hear it. i hope one day soon you will be able to stop
giving power to those who handicap you and do absolute
damage to your soul because they are able to manipulate
your emotions. there's a reason why they feed on you and
make you miserable, and it's not out of the love they have
for you. they need to starve you from the happiness you've
earned so they can attain the satisfaction from making you
suffer for their ineptitude for being human. nobody is
entitled to your life and no one is supposed to wear insults
and heinous remarks like souvenirs from an out of town
trip. we must remember that we are not what happens to
us, but what happens next that dictates who we become.
do not allow someone to choose that life for you. make
them see the difference before your back inevitably turns
into a crutch they can always lean on when they want
your best without them giving anything at all except a
heavy heart for you to hold in your chest.

in life, there are moments

i live and die for, and then

sometimes in-between,

i find enough courage to love

myself more than the times i

was in fear of it all.

i can feel the next fifty years by just laying with you
like this. i look at you and can see the room in my
heart where you'll always be, and no one could ever
replace your presence. i see her and know i want to
be the reason she loves life and laughs at the
randomness we encounter together. i've been
here before with you, and we were talking about
the same dreams we are living now. being connected
to you, i finally made sense of my hands, feet, heart,
purpose, and soul. for once you find that, you will never
lose yourself again. i know some people are not meant to
be in our lives forever, but don't take for granted the
ones that end up shaping who you are. they are the help
you don't have to cry out for, because pain is universal
and can paralyze you if it's left untreated. open yourself
up to the ones who love you and witness the chance.

i may be different, but she loves it,
and i'll take another fifty years if i
can have her.

no one can see you the way i do and i feel as if this is what i have been sent here for. not everyone gets to call you, beautiful, and in that sentiment alone, i am a mortal man living out his days unafraid of the truth that comes with knowing death. not everyone gets to hold you with arms that once had trouble fitting around his own potential. not everyone gets to kiss your fingertips and tell you how precious it is to have them touch me in the most honest and innocent of ways. not everyone gets to see you in the morning before you bring the sun to attention, while your eyes locate mine to make sure dreams are nothing more than a relationship with your soul. not everyone gets the pleasure of opening doors and pulling your chair out to let you know your presence is royal and you deserve every act of kindness i can facilitate for you. not everyone gets to see your bad days, the lost in thought moments, the tears behind the door, the collapsing to the floor, the difficult times, the not knowing what to do next instances, the joy from doing your best, the responsibility it takes being someone unearthly. no one gets to see that but me, and in those pictures i keep in my heart, i know why i was sent here. i know why loves means something with you. i know why life isn't the easiest of things to let play out, but to know you and love you, i have what i once couldn't understand all figured out. now we just have to keep it together for as long as we are able to look at each other with passion as if we are burning a hole into the sun, and we will make it to where one day, we'll give each other our final breath until we can do it all over again with what we have already been through. i will find you again, sweet one, because i'll never forget your favorite hiding spot behind the moon.

i am made from the scars
and memories before me,
but they do not tell the
entire story of the soul
that breathes inside.

they have loved me when
everyone left, and to me,
there is no greater friend
than that.

she keeps rocking that old school soul,
and it gives my heart the music it needs
to be able to succumb to her goddess-like
ways of transforming anything into
whatever she wants it to be.

swing with me from the galaxy around
us and don't let go until you hear the
sounds of insatiable laughter and
endless trails of stars.

that is where we will dance for the rest of time.

wash me
in your
darkness,
sweet one.

i want to
bathe in
your
skies.

the illusions before

me have always been

there, yet i am longing

for something more.

something

unattainable.

when you feel it coming and
you feel like you're closing
your mind to yourself,
open when ready.

      don't expedite the process.
      just follow the flowers and
      take their lead.

they all know when to bloom,
and not a second sooner
than needed.

we love like hands committed;
interlocking around the fire.

and like the fire, we bite at
every inch of skin exposed
to the dangers. we do this
because we aren't ourselves
anymore.

when before there was just an
"i" in front of me, now there
is a "you" to hold my body
back from being eaten alive
by the flames.

we go as one, even as ashes,
we rise again to taste the
wind. holding onto each
other, we are courageous
and undeniably something
infinite.

when i imagine you,
i run towards it with
my entire life.

if it isn't worth the breath
you cannot get back,
you shouldn't be
inhaling with
only half of
who you
are.

all i ask of you is
to trust the weight
inside that you feel
pressing your bones
flat.

> when you fall, you will
> only trust the one thing
> the birds do before flight;
> believing the wind is you.

to the military who have sacrificed family,
love, and life, thank you for what you do.
your constant bravery and unselfishness
is what this country represents.

to my brothers who i have bled with and
served with, thank you for being who
you are and teaching me the life
lessons it takes to be a better
man.

semper fi.

i love how you became my words when i had nothing left

to say or give to a world that took everything from me

without giving me a chance to say goodbye.

love is staying
in bed a few
extra hours
to watch the
sun rise
together on
the horizon
of where our
hearts always
meet.

you first spoke to me in a picture i saw.

you didn't know me then, but i knew

everything about you. it doesn't take

long to see the life you want, when the

person you can't live without is staring

back at you.

if i should ever

    breathe and your

        lips cannot feel it,

            i will know i am

                wasting my life

                    by not doing

                        the right thing.

all i want, is to love on you constantly for the
rest of my life. for those that never did before
me, thank you for allowing this angel into my
life and shame on you for not treating her
with more adoration and respect.

people tend to never appreciate the things
they don't understand or value more than
themselves.

> i will always hold you above
> the stars, sweet one.

little by little, this life is beginning to make sense.
where i thought i once would be, is not anywhere
that was intended for me. i do not play the games
most do. i don't have much to my name. but little
by little, this life of madness is growing inside of
me. it can be insane. it can be daunting. though
without my cracks, there would be no light for my
kind of love to shine through. so i will continue to
break down walls, until the only thing left inside is
the sun and a few clouds for shade. and when i am
tired, i will rest my head on the thought of your
name.

i used the moon as my sail, as i glided over the sea.
i wish you could've seen the stars in the ocean and
how brilliant everything appeared to be. as i made
my way to you, the whispering wind spoke out loud,
"a calm heart can make it through all the madness
lurking in the shadowy depths. now breathe with
the universe and you will find me."

we go in dreams as the night skies sing of hope and

beautiful things. calling out, we run without an

ounce of fear.

-the unknown awaits us-

i still remember the day you left and how my skin crawled
into the dark to go looking for my soul. on the days where
i thought i had the courage to move on was just a lie i had
to keep digesting to keep my eyes open. to keep my smile
up front and not behind the closed windows you locked
when you left. tomorrow there will be a likely scenario
of me seeing you or you seeing me and i am unsure if i
would say a goddamn thing to you. but if you ask me
tomorrow the same thing, i may change my mind. but
if you're happy to see me, then i will happily walk by
your life without asking for anymore of your time.
it's just that life wasn't supposed to be like this. it
was supposed to be our hands creating fire in the
sky.

time and time again, we get caught up in the now and not so much the next step. we argue with ourselves until there is no one left standing and we expect to make it where we thought we were destined to go before arrival. we must believe in not only our worth, but who we are as souls before anything else. what does that mean to you? what does that mean to your heart? if you cannot answer the question then you already know where to start and begin again.

it's not over after the fact. it's a continual process of

working and reworking yourself into your own life,

time and time again. we will only know each other

when it benefits the rest of our lives.

there are days when i swear
she knows what's going to
happen, and on the rare
occasion it doesn't go
according to plan,
it's the universe
being behind
again.

we exist to feel, and to not give yourself the simple

pleasures of life, you are leaving behind memories

you'll always wish you had. we exist, and it should

be without expectations, because once you have

them, you'll never be the same.

it was something you said and did every day that made my
mind fall asleep by just having you next to me. now i am
looking for a dream to stay in. a breath to believe in.
a heart to live in. maybe it's not worth the pain or
death of me to figure it out, but I will continue to
look for myself before love is found. where we go
from here is only the beginning and i hope it
starts as soon as i get out of this mess we call
a memory.

if it is destroying who you are, it isn't love, sweet child.
we must have enough power leftover to create something
we can grow with. we cannot continually give ourselves
to people in hopes of them fixing whatever we think is
wrong with who we are as humans. more than likely,
you've been told that all your life, and here you are,
still breaking for something that wasn't meant to
last, but you're still cutting your fingers on the
pieces, painting art they've never fucking
bothered looking at.

be bold enough to take back your life and heal
before giving your heart away again. rest it on
your values and sing it to sleep. it plays louder
for beautiful things, so be careful with all of
its strings. when ready, seek out your own
eyes first to see if it is love, or lust in
disguise.

you are proof that life will always
need a little extra adventure in
order to become meaningful.

without you and your
existence, it's to dull
to remember anything
at all. and what a

boring world it would be, if we were
content with loving things from afar,
without ever touching the sun or
jumping from waterfalls.

when i was younger, my love had corners folded into each

other. since i have met you, i've learned how to undo each

crease and lay out my heart perfectly. you made me forget

how to fold, and now it's a blanket we use to cover up

with.

our souls are only visitors to a body succumbed by earthly things. they venture out in silence, underneath the sights and sounds eating at us during the day.

a soul never forgets who touched it first, just as a human always remembers who found them before the moon did.

it was something different about the way she spoke.
you could taste the fragrance from her eyes and feel
the honey from her touch.

elegance and grace fell from her lips, just as the roses
in her throat could bloom when the moon showcased
her at night.

the truth about life is, we choose who we want, but more times than not, we hand that power over to someone who doesn't know how to handle us. we must learn to hold onto ourselves a little tighter and with more love.

it's the only way we will reach our own hearts before thinking another human knows how to care for it.

the sunset never

forgets where it

came from and

i will never deny

its power.

to the love of my life, who will never know how much she means to me, thank you, sweetheart, for always being my human journal when the paper couldn't understand the words.

i will marry you one day,
and it will be the end
of us being apart in
this lifetime.

she came into this world with
great love for broken things.
she always had that look of
help in her eyes that when
you saw it, you knew it was
okay to get back up,

and fight again.

with your tiny
hands in mine,
we climbed over
the wall separating
the earth and sea;
stealing all the stars
for you and me.

i love the last draw of breath
after the kiss. it's what makes
up everything else in the cosmos
around us. feel your lungs let go

and fall madly with
whatever comes next.

the question isn't about if she is worth it, because she is here with you now after all the bullshit and that should be the only reason needed for you to give your last breath fighting for her. think of how miserable life could be without her, when it's almost unbearable already.

you have your answer, but sometimes commitment is difficult and strenuous after never being able to love any part of yourself.

write to them.
write to her.
write to him.
write to who
you used to be.
and however
you get there,
write the ache out.

it doesn't deserve you anymore.

i was never suffering, sweet one.

i was merely awaiting your presence

in order to fulfill my purpose.

you're never too old to have your first love story

and you're never too young to begin something

that has the potential to last a lifetime.

say what you need to me.
do not hold anything back.
hiding what you feel kills
any chance you have at
happiness.

allow the flowers you keep
to breathe amongst the
free.

you are my favorite place to go in the whole universe.

if i get the honor of having you for the rest of my life,

i'll know how a human can finally shed his insecurities

and step out of his heart to feel the touch of something

wild and spontaneous.

she hides her face when she eats alone. buried deep
in her own thoughts and the eyes she feels around
her, she pretends to be somewhere else that doesn't
judge her for who she is. they don't know she goes
home by herself and barely understands the face
she sees. they don't know the struggle of love when
it had been non-existent her entire upbringing.
she doesn't harm herself anymore, because she
found the medicine needed in the poetry written
by those way before her time who died each day
so she could live right now. we all have our outlets,
but some choose to stay plugged into the notion
that everyone has to be equal or better than
someone else. when she leaves her house in the
morning, the streets are sleeping and the city
barely has a heartbeat. and on the days when
she sleeps in for a few extra hours, those same
city streets beg her for attention, pleading for
her to walk with them so they don't feel so
lonely. at the end of each day, all we can ask
for is that we did whatever we could to make
the best out of where we are at and make sure
we did our part in loving the fuck out of the
parts we keep in our pockets, hoping no one
has the courage to find them. she's getting
better, but like with most things, just needs
a little more time in the sun to grow.

we aren't indestructible, but we swear nothing can kills us twice. we are infatuated with broken things, and at the end of the day, there is great persistence to learn from it, as we conjure up enough courage to start again.

carry yourself with love and arrive.

you were not made to stay behind

the stars.

what is within you, has given me the ability to calm
the noise long enough to understand that i deserve
everything under the sky. but if for some reason that
doesn't come to be, being with you is the last and only
thing my heart needs to know.

one beat.

two beats.

three beats.

home.

i wish to only know you more. each day a deeper level.
each morning a new sound from you. each night a
new reason to make you smile. my hands will roll
over and move slowly to your face. i wish to hold
the moon and kiss it during each phase.

searching for some sort of sign, i look to you.

you are always there even if you're busy.

you take my hand and place it over my heart

when i am lost within this maze we call life.

it's only then do i feel its love.

i close my eyes and i see you smiling back.

your smile is my hope. it's the only thing

that truly knows me. the power it holds

when your cheeks meet mine as i kiss you

to thank you is something i hope continues

as our days grow together and last even longer.

my hands will never tire from tracing your outlines.
they will only grow stronger and softer for you as they
move down the moment.

you, my love, my sweetest deepest love, you have made
me believe all of us, each single atom, was created by the
kind of love poets can't drink to find and gods will never
understand.

and so we continue to fly on wings of love
and desire for something we can call our
own. we adventure with hearts made from
endless dreams and a resiliency bathed in
stardust. we are the world inside ourselves
that never stops rotating for all things
precious and meaningful. we are a bed
that never gets made, but when i am with
you, nothing needs to be perfect. that's who
i fell in love with and that's who i hold when
there are no covers left when we're out of breath.

wherever we go, let's always kiss each other when we can
and swing from the moon every night. i have never had
anyone like you. i have never had anything like us.

      sunsets were made to be felt,
      and our love is no different.

we all have hearts born in different places.

we all have experiences that age the soul.

we all have a story to tell, and i hope you

get the courage to tell it when you're ready.

i've spent a lifetime chasing adventures
to talk about when i am old and grey.

i just hope you are there to help me
remember the good parts.

be more you.

the world loves when you show your bones.
the flesh is merely hiding your true beauty.

you will be the reason why i never
give up trying to win over the stars.

we shall walk barefoot across the
night sky onto our next adventure.

you, me, a blanket, and nothing
else but the moon.

the only things you need
when love is what you're
after.

there is something sexy about a human who can take
you to the moon without ever leaving your bed and
talk about how being next to you is all they ever need
on their bad days.

crazy hearts always find each other in a wild world.

all day long i have been thinking about what it must feel like for others who go without someone like you. the moment our eyes met, the universe grew and time failed to move without us.

life goes better with you, love.

we love as if we have known each other before.
back when our hands were curators for the sun
and moon. back when we spoke in galaxies and
constellations. back when our souls were free
from bodily form.

      we will love today.
      we will love tomorrow.
      we will love, again and again.

      there is nothing else but to love
      when you've been away for this
      long.

when a laugh turns into a reason for falling in love and wanting to give your best self to them, you will be at the doorstep of the first and last thing you'll wish to ever be a part of.

together, you will have the stars reaching out for you.

all around me there are pieces of you etched into the walls of those who seek a different form of love.

-a kind that separates flesh from soul-no matter what you look or feel like. no matter what you are experiencing, i will love you through it and be there to tell you how proud i am of you. standing there, embracing your questions and concerns, i have an arm full of flowers needing to open. i will wait patiently for you to speak in yellows, reds, and blues about your day. i will be there every goddamn time. once you take a deep breath with me, we will move forward, together.

i miss you when you sleep. my day doesn't start until you tell me, "good morning lover."

those words are the catalyst for my heart to awake and bring its love to you. i watch you sleep, because i still haven't figured out how lungs as soft as yours create the rise and fall in my soul. the way you move it without moving a single limb of your own, you move me closer to that spot on your shoulder where i go to wait for you.

please, my love,

tell me again how you were scattered by the stars.

when you are not beside me, i am lost to a space without your soul. the air around me thickens and becomes unhealthy to the art of me. always be at least a whisper away, darling.

there is nothing greater than knowing you are loved

the same by someone who gave you permission to

finally accept it for yourself.

there are places i'll never go and roads
i'll never travel, but your hands, breasts,
and lips are destinations that will always
have my soul.

explore. explore. explore.

i am nothing more than a
feather caught in the wind,

but still, i fly.

the greatest form of love you will ever find is someone who wants nothing more than to hold you when you feel your tears cutting rivers into your bones. you will begin to understand that it's okay to be at your lowest when someone doesn't mind floating with you for a little while until your soul comes back to rest.

souls touching and hearts embracing...

that's how galaxies collide.

with eyes protruding flowers, she speaks easy
about the petals falling, knowing they will be
safe where they belong. she is comfortable in
her art and in the openness of her space.

creativity is her language as she speaks
of a foreign tongue no longer known
by the humans around her. an old soul
caught in a modern world, she's anchored
to her own heart, but lives in the moments
no one else pays attention to. those are the
ones she holds close at night, resuscitating
the sky, one star at a time.

chaos exists to keep balance between your feet and the earth. its freewill creates all that you see and everything which is made to kill you. death is nothing more than a slow pulse waiting for lightning to kiss it.

-you get to choose which madness you will live for-

being different has been the greatest teacher,
and i remain this way because of those who
taught me to laugh at everything while
maintaining love for yourself,
regardless of the ache tap
dancing in your heart.

we get lost because we much rather be somewhere else
than wherever we are now. take the chance to fly.

take the chance to give meaning to your life besides
the countless excuses you use not to try.

even if the sky did fall,
i would still be under
it with you.

and after all the chaos,
we would still have the
stars on our side.

you can spill your soul to me and not worry
about cleaning anything. life was made to be
messy, sweetheart.

tonight, we are letting them run over the edge.

she forgave me for my scars and i ultimately learned how

to forgive myself. this kind of love teaches you how to

overcome your past by having your future present

every day you are alive.

life is a bit of a mess, but if you can find someone

who stands in front of it all, making love the focal

point, everything will be where it is supposed to be.

you are a phenomenon and so unearthly profound.
i close my eyes and see you as a single smile in a
crowd of a thousand frowns.

you have an unorthodox approach to life and i
cannot help but to fall harder in love with you.

especially when you wear nothing at all.

sometimes i say too much and other times i can go days
without saying a single word. regardless of the situation,
you're all i can think about, and it is beautiful.

my hands feel like lost children, abandoned by their home
when they are not on you or holding yours. they don't
know where to go and are wandering for the entire
duration you're gone.

                         now tired and motionless by
                         my side, they wait and hang
                         on for you.

with bare bones and all, she flies. left with nothing, she turned it into a reality she was always prohibited from seeing. she only belongs to herself now, and for that reason alone, her freedom feels better than any company who can't make her feel secure. in her eyes is where the pain sleeps, but it's at night you can tell the strength in her heart. the kind of resilience that can move the moon for those who need it most.

it wasn't her laugh that got me nor was it her smile. it was
the simple fact of me telling her my story and her saying,
"thank you." i knew then i would never be the same
person i was this morning, staring hopelessly into
a mirror that wouldn't talk back and refused to
believe in the good things i had always told
others.

each time she speaks,
a layer of me is pulled
back softly.

not everyone has had
the opportunity to be
loved while having a
naked heart and soul,
but if you do, let go.

there's magic in the remains.
there's peace in the pieces.
there's melody in the chaos.
there's hope in the fall.

if you ever get the chance,
give yourself up to the
hands who want only yours
to hold. maybe the spaces fit
and maybe they don't, but at
least it's a connection to
someone who wants to try
to make it work.

you can go too long with them
being empty and they will begin
to reject anything that looks like
effort.

you are the greatest love i know. now i understand how the
sun feels when it touches the moon. it's because of you i
don't feel the war inside of me anymore. it's because of
you that the rage turned into feathers which i now use
to rest the dead i had been carrying.

you are the greatest friend i know. now i understand how
anxiety can be forgotten when it had been the only thing
i thought would never leave me. it's because of you my
mind can fathom a future without worrying about the
ghosts that had been renting out space to make me a
shell of who i needed to be.

you alone could bring peace to this crazy world,
but you've given it all to me.

it's okay to be emotional and have a deep
love for something , for those who tell
you differently, remove them from your
life. they are the ones who probably think
someone smiling at them means they are
flirting and then get pissed off because
they weren't.

life is about perspective and balance.
if you have one without the other,
you are going to stay irritated and
ignore the boundaries someone
set up long before you arrived.

people are lessons and i hope you
learn how to separate yourself from
those being neglectful to themselves
from the ones who absolutely mean
what they say.

before you say anything, you are necessary in my life. i'll need you, but not suffocate you. i've never been able to fully write down everything you have done for me, because that is an impossible feat, but i will continue to try my best to love you with what the universe has given to me. when i tell you how much you've impacted my life, just know my world means nothing without you by my side. i speak of you often as if you put the moon in my sky, when in reality, you're everything above me. lifetimes will reach out to us for answers on how we are doing this together, and i will tell them it has been achieved by believing in something more than just us. there's an idea everyone has of how it's supposed to be, when all you have to do is love each other in the sincerest of forms. sometimes a note in the morning changes their entire day and it's within that moment you read words you had never heard before. spontaneity goes a long way when you're trying to build from what others couldn't understand or didn't want to know completely. venture outside of what has been the norm for you and fixate everything you have on a few seconds of bravery, and you will spend the rest of your life knowing you took that chance when you thought there were none left to seize. love is funny, but she is the laughter i will always need. my lungs have gone too long not knowing how to inhale and exhale properly, but now it is her soul who breathes for me.

we exist so others can believe in life after the pain.

somewhere in the middle we figure out how

susceptible it is to fall for everything that makes

us who we are. there is nothing more daring than

getting up as many times as it takes with what

you've learned.

i see where all things come to live and die. where the universe's roof keeps everything you love covered and allows you to see the beauty underneath the skies we call home. all too often i feel out of place, a common stranger to an uncommon world. i have been misplaced by purpose. i am awkward around anything living. i am shy when there's no one around and i'm talking to myself. i am here, and i have more good days than bad, so i know how fortunate it is to write my own version of what i see and feel, hoping others can find something in it to hold onto while living theirs.

there's this story about a woman who kept trying to figure
out where she was and how to get away. i could see it in
her doll like eyes that she had invented herself so well,
she couldn't escape the masquerade of her own heart.
it weighed heavily on her soul and one day she took a
rope and tied it to her vertebrae and scaled down her
face. she's strange, eccentric, and completely mad, but
i loved her fighting spirit and how she survived in almost
certain death. it takes that kind of woman to be with me
because i too had to runaway from myself to find who i
was supposed to be.

i love you means i know and i am staying. if something
should not go the way we would like it to, i will take the
place of the sun and you will take over for the moon,
and we will rise to see each other to try again. life is
about the difficult times that either keep you where
you are or make you strong enough to finally say goodbye.
balance is only met when you are done sacrificing yourself
for the betterment of any situation you are in. be mindful,
but never lose your identity for someone who thinks it is
okay to call you a different name every time you forget to
do something. love never tells you it's going to work, it just
gives you an opportunity to try and make it last. the only
way to know, is if you are honest before it begins.

i'll suffer in your silence because i don't want you feeling as if you have to do it alone. my energy will be reflected by yours and if it drags me down, so be it. i'd rather sit with you and say nothing than be away and not know where you are. if we are honest with ourselves, we will be bleed the truth like the moon does every night as it shows us what we need when we need it. i have a transcendent love affair with it each time she opens up a new part of me i had nailed and bolted shut; unwilling to let anyone see the disasters i've been keeping to myself. no one deserves to be mauled by them, but she matches her scars with mine and it is then i know i've never been alone. i have had the most sincerest experience of getting to know her beyond the surface so many others think they can trace with their eyes closed, when i can draw her with my heart. there's something to be said about someone that allows you access to your own struggles by being the reason you no longer have to worry about them going unnoticed and without the essence of love. they will be the catalyst to every goddamn thing you ever wanted to do but couldn't because you were holding yourself back due to the fact you forgot where you placed your dreams.

she loved herself back to life after being emotionally
abused for so long. it never became physical even
though the threats were becoming more severe.
she considers herself lucky knowing how badly it
has ended for others who thought change was
coming, only to be greeted with a cold shoulder
and a door slamming in her face. she wondered
if it was her own doing that he didn't love her.
she thought it was her fault he stayed gone until
four or five in the morning. after the last altercation,
she gathered all of what was left of her, and moved on.
it took months to get back who she was before the
monster told her things he knew she wanted to hear.
she is prospering now and has a family with one daughter.
each morning before she drops her off at school, she hugs
her, and says, "know that i love you and don't ever stop
counting your smiles. they are just as important as
heartbeats."

i hope you find someone who is willing to become
everything you've never had. i hope you find someone
who helps you around the house without having to say
a single word. and if they were to say something, i hope
it's, "i've already finished that for you." i hope you see
the true meaning in the way humans are supposed to
love without fear of losing themselves, because with
love, comes the possibility of losing everything.
i hope you find someone who understands the
concept and idea of what companionship honestly
is. i hope you never lose your passion for becoming
who you need, because once you do, you'll be another
sad face and set of longing eyes hanging on someone's
wall. don't be the one who fights to stay where there is
nothing left to be loved, because you will always carry
the war with you after everything has been destroyed.
we all hope to find someone who gets us, and when
you feel like you have exhausted every option, love
yourself more.

there's a reason for her quietness. if you are trying to help, all you have to do is sit, learn, and listen. it will take you inside of your own madness of which you were too scared to venture into alone. when she speaks, when she is ready to open her heart, that's when the awakening begins. be prepared to fall in love with her sincere sense of wonder. allow her to take you where she is going. the only thing you should be worried about, is if you brought enough magic to match hers. they don't hand out dreams to just anyone these days. they are earned through agonizing lessons of being left by those you never thought would leave and thinking you were never good enough for the unbelievable parts of life. you don't have to follow each footstep she makes, but if you want to see the universe as it should be seen, step gently into her passion for adventure and you will find yourself at the edge of the trees, looking down at a waterfall spilling off the side of the world you thought didn't exist. eyes are merely mirrors for the lost who only have the urge to discover more of what others aren't looking for. take a handful of stars and wash them off from time to time. she will teach you things, and most importantly, she will introduce you to who you were meant to be.

i love people who get excited about doing something they've never done before. the ones who cannot help but laugh at themselves no matter who's in the room. the ones that can sit and watch certain people around them and be in awe of their ability to be happy by not needing anything more than just a few more seconds of a thought. the ones who get lost in everything they do because they cannot see themselves anywhere else, with anyone else, putting together a scrapbook filled with paper hearts cut out of the universe. i love people for the most part, and it's why writing has always been my form of communication since an early age. i never looked for a connection with the energy around me, but i found myself involved everywhere i was. there is this instinct to feel regardless of my own emotions, and because of that, i've been able to mature in a place that applauds and idolizes those who aren't. i don't mind people not caring about me or what i do. i don't mind people pretending they don't see me as i see myself. i don't mind people frantically searching for something to believe in so they can do whatever they want and then think they will be forgiven. you see, all i care about is making sure i don't become them. i enjoy being a creation of every part of the world i have been to. it has taught me how being alive is enough and the rest is a made up belief that it isn't. we don't always need more. we just need to make where we are better for those behind us.

there are so many things that are new to me since being
with you. but if you were to ask me which one means
the most, i would have to say myself. before you, i hated
everything i was. i didn't value this soul. i never smiled
and meant it. i guess you could say i was happy, but not
because i chose it. when you find yourself rolling over
and hesitating before pulling back the covers she stole,
it makes sense to stay awake for those few moments
before doing so in order to savor how it is to be in love.
maybe you don't do anything but lay there, wrapped up
like a kiss in the wind, enjoying her presence, but love
never holds it breath to make you wonder. it all comes
natural when love is in your heart because you choose
to let it walk around, accompanied by poetry that was
written for her before you two even spoke. to see ink
turn into flesh, and for it to belong to you, that's
something i can live for.

somewhere between dylan and petty,
her life was discovered.

she's an american girl who dreams in
lyrics of the songs she has memorized
and each place that has had the honor
of hosting her heart for the night.
there's a sweet romance to be had
when the night becomes your
friend and tells you about the secrets
it shares with the lost moon children
wandering amongst the wolves.
continue walking with a light heart,
sweet child. only allow the best parts
of life to fill it up. anything else will
choke your dreams in the middle of
your sleep and you'll wake up covered
with the tears of everything that could
have been. being this way has taught her
how to fall in love with an adventure
instead of humans that are only looking
out for themselves. we go in search of
something we can call our own, and it's
beyond our fears where we find a kind
of wild that knows us by our first name,
and loves us for our bravery.

i will need you in the most softest of ways on days
i am feeling worthless. i will cradle all of your hurt
when you are breaking, because someone like you
shouldn't have to cry alone. i will be the center of
your circle, and together, we will take on whatever
comes next. we will not be defined by our wounds.
we will be remembered for overcoming them.

even though i was raised by uncertainty, i will never
make you second guess what you mean to me. i will
exhaust every ounce of who i am to give you
something you've never had.